CW00408892

JANICE M. BOSTOK

Dimmed the Mystery

SNAPSHOT PRESS

First published 2000 by
Snapshot Press
PO Box 132
Crosby
Liverpool
L23 8XS
England

A CIP record for this book
is available from the British Library

Printed in England

Design and layout by John Barlow

Front cover photograph
Campbell's Lane, Dungay, New South Wales
by Janice M. Bostok

Photograph of author by Bruce Devine

ISBN 0 9526773 2 6

To my husband Silvester
who suffered a stroke
on 29 May 1998

Acknowledgements

Thanks are due to the editors and publishers of the following publications in which some of these poems previously appeared:

Hobo, Paper Wasp, Snapshots, Social Alternatives, Tangled Hair, Tanka Splendor 1998 (AHA Books, 1998) and *Valley Vibrations*.

Awards

'determined':
Tanka Splendor Award, 1998

This collection was a runner-up in the
Snapshots Collection Competition 1999.

lone gull's cry
enters my grey day
forlorn i ponder
on the gregarious flocks
dropping from sunnier skies

caterpillars
eat enormous amounts
but for the emerging moth
and i when confronting you
there is no useful mouth

autumn evening
doves peck amongst
driveway gravel
for seeds thrown to appease
my melancholy mood

in that briefly
illuminating flash
an implosion
dissolves my tension
into liquefied anguish

your silent anger
festering in summer heat
flattens my joyous spirits
as it does the ears
of our cautious cat

wanting to be closer
to you i walk the land
where we once worked
together tending vines
and harvesting the fruit

aged now
and dimmed the mystery
which lured me around
each bend in the country lane
of the district which i call home

as a mouse seen
from the corner of the eye
in autumn   you too
need to winter for another
season in this old house

purple swamp hen
uses the footbridge to cross
unlike i who have
no way to help you make
the transition to old age

determined
crow pecks holes in a plastic
garbage bag
unrewarded as i in breaking
through your silence

together
yet no steady gaze holds
our separateness
in half forgotten sorrows
of first time married life

i know they're out there
those mammoths of the deep
but only when they breach
am i reminded
of our young lovemaking ways

since your illness
the sad joy of lovemaking
is more traumatic
than the wild passions
we once regularly shared

from afar
storm beginnings rumble
closer & closer
a flash of memory
heals my desperate need

in half sleep
an involuntary orgasm
more gentle
as you have been
since your stroke

before leave-taking
dawn pinks silver birch trails
unnoticed
on other mornings not touched
by wind without promise

in another land
roommate sleeps naked
aviary birds waken
muffled cries of loneliness
stifled by memories of you

raging sou'westerly
above its fearful roar
i hear your voice
rattling the window frames
calling me back home

in a foreign land
zoo orang-utans groom
each other closely
my thoughts return home
your cancer is in remission

alone this night
you don't come as once when walls
were for walking through
and obstacles were footballs
for kicking goals

white throated nightjar
shatters my bedroom's
deep silence
in the healing process i cross
the dark hallway to your room

cemetery hill
quickens my love
still growing
wild as green grasses
on an unmarked grave

dead now
i still cup the baby bird
in my hands
the cold shudder i feel
is hopelessness for us

banana plants
no longer in regimented
rows on the hillsides
unravel your ordered days
the wanting for death begun

cloud ablaze
its light streams a halo
over the mountain
our breasts heave
in unison

hypnotic lapping
of a flat surf lulls me
into believing
the sea's depth is harmless
as once your love also was

i voice opinion
and like the unwanted
note of discord
it cannot be returned
to the hollowed instrument

our new kitten
mouths a silent cry
ineffectual
as your own voice
since your paralysing stroke

returned
to my home at sunset
poinciana blooms
cloak the town
in a dense red haze

kitten
chews on a dead bird
the stiff legs move
jerk haltingly as yours
affected by your stroke

watching tv
your hand on my thigh
pulls me warmly
back into past moments
that we have shared

saved from the cat
i enclose it in my hand
think on its brightness
as it flitted through the blue
awake it grips my finger

breathtaking
the silver & black pattern
of the old cedar
how delicate your face
in the moonlight tonight

night
without movement
bagpipe notes
stir the rhythms
of my ancestors

you cling to me
as i imagine a woman
might do
yet your body feels
more manly in its yielding

your breath
is the sound of newly emerged
butterfly wings
leisurely expanding
on a sun-warmed blossom bough

you hospitalised
for one month i walk
our empty house
unfamiliar in its fullness
of winter cold

no one to tend
the vegetable garden
no green tomatoes
sitting on the windowsill
the cat stretches & yawns

you offer me
the new moon in a dusky sky
as if it were a piece
of some treasure you'd found
and thought to share with me

night is your longed for
soft silken coffin lining
another dawning
light bright sunshine stimulates
life for one more day

mourning you
so many times in life
i try to imagine
what it will really be like
when you are gone in death

she comes to me
in silence and in stealth
and when she pounces
into my lap   i know
i still can fall in love

white heron
returned from feeding grounds
at dusk
lightens the darkening sky
of my homeward journey

unbelievingly
it has come to this
a slow release
from my former self is worse
than the quick jolt of death

By the same author

Banana Leaves (Self-published, Australia, 1972)

Walking into the Sun (Shelters Press, USA, 1974)

Hearing the Wind (Self-published, Australia, 1976)

On Sparse Brush (Makar Gargoyle Poets Series, Australia, 1978)

Silver Path of Moon (PostPressed, Australia, 1996)

Still Waters (EarthDance, Australia, 1997)

The Farmer Tends His Land (Tiny Poems Press, USA, 1997)

Shadow-Patches (Hallard Press, New Zealand, 1998)

A Splash of Sunlight (Self-published, Australia, 1998)

About the Author

Janice M. Bostok was born in Mullumbimby, New South Wales in 1942. She began writing haiku in 1971, and edited and published the magazine *Tweed* from 1972 to 1979. Since 1994 she has co-edited *Paper Wasp*, and she was also the haiku adviser for *Hobo* from 1995 to 1999. An experienced contest adjudicator and workshop leader, her own haiku and tanka have been published extensively around the world and have won numerous awards. A number of her haiku have also recently been carved on rocks in a park in Katikati, New Zealand, as part of the town's Millennium Project. Since arriving as newly weds over thirty years ago, she has lived with her husband on Campbell's Lane, a gravel road winding up into the hills from the closest town. The title poem of this, her first collection of tanka, was written about this lane.

For details of other haiku-related books and journals published by Snapshot Press, including other titles in this chapbook series, please send an s.a.e. (+ 1 IRC internationally) to the address on page 2.